for a
Wonderful Friend
365 Little Encouragements

Inspired by Faith

For a Wonderful Friend
ISBN 978-0-9848369-4-9

Published by Product Concept Mfg., Inc.
2175 N. Academy Circle #200, Colorado Springs, CO 80909

©2012 Product Concept Mfg., Inc. All rights reserved.

All scripture quotations are from the King James version
of the Bible unless otherwise noted.

Scriptures taken from the Holy Bible,
New International Version®, NIV®.
Copyright © 1973, 1978, 1984 by Biblica, Inc.™
Used by permission of Zondervan.
All rights reserved worldwide.
www.zondervan.com

Sayings not having a credit listed are contributed by writers
for Product Concept Mfg., Inc. or in a rare case,
the author is unknown.

Written and Compiled by Vicki Kuyper
in association with Product Concept Mfg., Inc.

for a
Wonderful Friend

A friend loveth at all times.
Proverbs 17:17

YOU'RE A
WONDERFUL FRIEND...

the kind who showers kindness into the lives of others. It's time to pour a little refreshment back into your own life. In the morning, in the evening, or anytime in between, soak in these words of encouragement. Let them lighten your heart, strengthen your resolve and stir your soul—365 days a year.

THIS WORLD'S MORE BEAUTIFUL
BECAUSE OF YOU

1 There never has been—and never will be—another you. Your smile, your personality, your gifts and your love change this world for the better each day. Revel in your individuality!

"A FRIEND IS A GIFT
YOU GIVE YOURSELF."

Robert Louis Stevenson

2 Do yourself a favor: risk reaching out to a stranger. You never know when you'll meet a "friend for life."

LIGHTEN YOUR EMOTIONAL LOAD

3 When past hurts or regrets weigh you down, unpack your emotional baggage. Grieve, forgive, make amends and take to heart lessons learned. Then, move on. Refuse to drag the past along with you into the future.

IT'S NICE TO SAY "NO"

Give yourself a chance to say "no" before you say "yes." Your time, energy, resources and emotions have limits. Respect them.

4

WALK A MILE IN HER PEEP TOES

Every life is a balance of blessings and challenges. All you can read from where you stand is the cover of another woman's life. Remember, there's always more to her story— and yours—than meets the eye.

5

TREAT YOURSELF
TO AN INSTANT FACELIFT

Smile! It's been scientifically proven that smiling improves your mood. It can also help brighten the day of those who cross your path. So, go ahead…give in and grin.

6

SHIFT YOUR FOCUS

7

Instead of measuring your lifestyle with that of the rich and famous, focus more on those less fortunate. As your gratitude for your own blessings grows, you'll find yourself more inspired to share, than compare.

"VOYAGE, TRAVEL AND CHANGE OF PLACE IMPART VIGOR"
Seneca

8

If you need a vacation but can't get away, take a mental flight of fancy. Plan a trip to somewhere in preparation for someday. Savor the anticipation.

GIVE YOURSELF A DO-OVER

You're a wonderfully gifted woman, but you're also human. That means you'll make mistakes. View each misstep as an opportunity for growth. Then, pick yourself up and start again.

TICKLE YOUR FUNNYBONE

Giggle, guffaw, chuckle and snort (if you must!). Laughter brings out the kid in you as it washes away the stress of the day. Look for the humor hiding all around you.

USE THE NEWS

11

Whether you hear, watch or read the daily news, it can leave you feeling helpless. You can't save the world, but you can make a positive change. Volunteer when you can, pray when you can't and choose to share "good" news with those around you.

REFLECT LESS ON YOUR REFLECTION

12

A mirror can't show you who you really are. The affirming words of those who love you paint a more accurate picture. Let your friends help you see the true you more clearly.

STOP AND SMELL
THE CINNAMON ROLLS

Take time to savor your meals. Chew slowly. Enjoy the variety of flavors, textures and aromas. This practice aids in digestion and helps you recognize more easily when you're full, so you'll eat only what you need.

13

"WHEREVER YOU ARE,
BE ALL THERE."
Jim Elliott

Whether you're in a time of abundance or need, celebration or sorrow, today only comes around once. Refuse to live life on autopilot. Grab hold of the lessons it has to teach so you won't have to relearn them tomorrow.

14

THE CHOICE IS YOURS

15 Today, will you be kind? Share words that heal, instead of those that hurt? Live within your means? Nurture a grudge or set it free? Each day you choose how you will live— and how you'll love. Choose wisely.

JUST DO IT

16 Every woman faces tasks, decisions or relational issues she'd rather ignore. But ignoring something unpleasant doesn't make it disappear. It makes life more stressful. Do yourself a favor today by doing one thing you've been putting off.

BUY THE SIZE THAT FITS

Your beauty and worth cannot be gauged by the size on a label. They're beyond measure. What fits, flatters—regardless of size.

17

THERE'S NO PLACE LIKE HOME...
REALLY

Regardless of how long you've lived at your present address, there's always more to explore. Take a hike. Try a new restaurant. Venture down an unknown street. Discover what sets your corner of the world apart from the rest.

18

SPEAK UP

19

You have a unique perspective on the world.
That's why sharing your point of view is so
valuable. Refuse to bury your opinions,
even when you know others may disagree.
Listen attentively. Then respond respectfully.
Your voice deserves to be heard.

YOU'RE IN WONDERFUL COMPANY

20

You are an interesting woman. Even when
you're alone, there's no need for you to feel
lonely. There's always more you can discover
about yourself. Journal, putter in the garden,
allow your mind to wander and pay attention to
where it leads.

> ## "AN ADVENTURE IS ONLY
> ## AN INCONVENIENCE
> ## RIGHTLY CONSIDERED."
> ### *G. K. Chesterton*

21

When your plans are interrupted by the unexpected you have two choices. You can sit and stew over what might have been or head a new direction. Who knows? The latter may lead you somewhere you've always wanted to go.

KNOCK DOWN YOUR OWN FENCES

22

Do you ever feel you're "not enough"? Not pretty enough. Smart enough. Good looking enough. Charming enough…You fill in the blank. Lies you tell yourself can fence in your future. Focus on what you are—you're so much more than just "enough."

SAY "I LOVE YOU" OUT LOUD

Sure, your friends and family know you love them. But there's still something powerful about saying those three words aloud. They're a gift that's a joy to both give and receive. Give them away today.

23

FIND YOUR MUSE

24

What gets your creative juices flowing?
Music? Visiting an art gallery? Basking in the
glory of nature? Traveling an unknown road?
Schedule some time today to invite your muse
to come out and play.

"GENIUS IS ONE PERCENT INSPIRATION AND 99 PERCENT PERSPIRATION."
Thomas Edison

25

Edison tried 10,000 ways to create the light
bulb. Every failure taught him something that
brought him closer to success. Don't give up.
There's genius in you.

EXERCISE YOUR MATERNAL INSTINCTS

26

Whether you're a mother or not, you can
lavish the children around you with love. Every
child needs a circle of grownups who believe
in them, who tell them the truth about who
they are: that they're beautiful, brave and
uniquely significant.

"ALL I HAVE SEEN TEACHES ME
TO TRUST THE CREATOR
FOR ALL I HAVE NOT SEEN."
Ralph Waldo Emerson

27

The diversity, complexity and meticulous order of the natural world are a reminder that there's more to this life than you can see with your eyes. Embrace the wonder and mystery that surround you.

GIVE YOURSELF
THE SILENT TREATMENT

28

Take a break from the TV, radio, computer and cell phone for at least a few hours today. By getting comfortable with silence you give your thoughts a chance to be heard. You may be surprised with what you hear.

COLOR OUTSIDE THE LINES

29

Shake up your daily routine by trying something new. Prepare a new recipe. Taste a new food. Read a book outside your usual genre. Try on a style you'd usually pass by. You may discover a few new favorites.

REWRITE YOUR STORY

30

If you don't like the direction your life is headed, make a change. Break a habit. Go back to school. Take positive steps toward becoming the parent, wife or friend you've always wanted to be. Let your happily ever after begin today.

"BELIEF IS A TRUTH HELD IN THE MIND; FAITH IS A FIRE IN THE HEART."
Joseph Fort Newton

31

Faith acts on what it believes. If what you believe to be true—about God or yourself—has no affect on your life, it's nothing more than a positive thought.

PUT YOURSELF IN TIME OUT

Feeling overscheduled and overstressed? Breathe. Literally. Give yourself and your body a break by closing your eyes and breathing deeply for a few moments. Pray, if you like. Then start afresh and do what needs to be done.

32

BASK IN THE WONDER OF "YOU"

Consider the intricate miracle of the body and brain you have the privilege of using each day. Ponder each breath, heartbeat and wiggle of your toes. Be gentle in the way you treat such an extraordinary piece of art.

33

BE THE FRIEND YOU WANT TO HAVE

Think of what you look for in a true friend. Then be that kind of friend to others. Your circle of friends is sure to grow larger and deeper.

34

35

"ONLY THOSE WHO RISK GOING TOO FAR CAN POSSIBLY FIND OUT HOW FAR THEY CAN GO."
T. S. Eliot

Push beyond the physical, mental and spiritual boundaries you usually live within. You're stronger, smarter and more deeply loved than you could ever imagine.

36

TREAT YOURSELF TO SOME ZZZZZZS

A well-rested body is better prepared to face the mental, physical and emotional challenges of a new day. Go to bed fifteen minutes earlier tonight or nab a brief nap when you can. Pamper yourself with a chance for sweet dreams.

37

PERFECT THE ART OF IMPERFECTION

You're a strong, intelligent woman. But you do have weaknesses. Everyone does. The more familiar you are with your Achilles heel the easier it is to work around it or work toward strengthening it.

PREPARE FOR GENEROSITY

Choose to live a bit below your means.
It not only gives you a financial cushion to lean
on in case of emergency, but enables you to
give more generously and spontaneously when
you see a need arise.

38

BE AN "ARMS OPEN WIDE" RECEIVER

It's humbling to be on the receiving end
of a gift. But it's part of the give and take of
being in relationships. Graciously accepting
what others give to you and do for you is one
very important way of saying, "Thanks."

39

"CHARACTER IS WHAT YOU ARE
IN THE DARK."
Dwight L. Moody

A woman of integrity is the same person in
public that she is when no one's watching.
Allowing the true you to shine through in any
and every situation makes you a woman worthy
of respect.

40

YOU'RE NEVER TOO OLD
TO BE A CHEERLEADER

41

To encourage others literally means to help build hope, confidence and courage into their lives. Be liberal with compliments and stingy with criticism. Encouraging the best in others will also bring out the best in you.

CELEBRATE THE SEASON YOU'RE IN

42

Every age has its benefits and its challenges. Focus on how far you've come, instead of what you've left behind. You only get one shot at being the age you are today.

QUESTION YOUR CRAVINGS

43

When it's hard to say "No" to something you want, ask yourself "Why?" before you indulge. Snarfing a brownie or buying a new pair of shoes will never fill your deepest longings. Ask God to help you find what you're really searching for.

MOVE TO THE MUSIC

Snow White's dwarves knew the secret to
getting a job done: whistle while you work.
So, crank up the music. Dance and sing
(or whistle) your way through your chores.
You'll be finished before you know it.

44

DON'T WORRY, BE PRAYERFUL

Worry is a thought that's headed the wrong
direction. It's focused inward, instead of
upward. Change what you can and let God
handle the rest by turning every worry into
a prayer that you lift up to Him.

45

UNTANGLE FAMILY TIES

When rifts or misunderstandings occur,
refuse to sweep them under the rug. Reconcili-
ation requires honest communication. Get the
conversation started by extending love and
grace where it's needed most.

46

"LIFE IS EITHER A DARING ADVENTURE OR NOTHING."
Helen Keller

47

Life is full of opportunities, invitations to push yourself beyond the limits of your comfort zone. Take one of your "maybe someday" dreams and bring it one step closer to becoming reality.

NURTURE YOUR SPIRITUAL SIDE

48

You are a spiritual person. Your longing for purpose, peace and a life that continues after death is hard-wired into who you are. Listen for God's whisper, reminding you there's more to life than can be seen with your eyes.

BE A BLESSING

It's as easy as opening a door for a mom whose hands are full or as challenging as using your vacation time to help feed the homeless. When you see a need, consider how you can help. You could be God's answer to someone's prayer.

49

USE THE GOOD CHINA

Why should holidays get all of the attention? Acknowledge the personal victories and unexpected joys found in an ordinary day. Celebrating the little things will help you realize they're not so little after all.

50

"TIME YOU ENJOYED WASTING IS NOT WASTED TIME."
T. S. Eliot

There's a time to work hard and a time to sit back and celebrate all you've accomplished. Relax. Let your mind wander. Bask in the beauty of a lazy day.

51

THERE'S NO EXPIRATION
DATE ON FRIENDSHIP

52

Friends will move in and out of your life as you change your address, your job or your stage of life. That doesn't make them obsolete. Reconnect with an old friend. Rediscover the joy of shared memories as you create new ones.

BECOME A LIFELONG STUDENT

53

You don't have to be in school to learn something new. Cultivate your curiosity. Learn a foreign language. Master an unfamiliar skill. Read. Explore. Listen to what others have to teach. There's always more to learn.

LIVE TODAY, TODAY

54

You may not be looking forward to tomorrow. Perhaps there's an upcoming obligation or confrontation you'd rather not face. Don't let tomorrow use up today. You'll do what needs to be done when the time comes.

SEND OUT AN S.O.S.

Need help? Ask for it. Part of the joy of a relationship is helping one another. Where one is weak, the other is strong. Your opportunity to answer another's S.O.S will come soon enough.

55

GO THE EXTRA MILE

Take the stairs instead of the elevator. Park at the back of the lot. Turn off the TV or computer and take a walk around the block. Adding extra steps to your day is always a healthy move.

56

LOVE EXTRAVAGANTLY

To love without expecting anything in return doesn't mean inviting others to "use" you. It simply means continuing to give your best, even when others fail. Love that doesn't keep score is love in the truest sense of the word.

57

HUMILITY IS LIFE'S REALITY CHECK

58

A humble woman sees herself for who she really is. She can accept both criticism and praise because she's fully aware of both her strengths and her weaknesses. She sees herself through God's eyes. Do you?

"THE REAL VOYAGE OF DISCOVERY CONSISTS NOT IN SEEKING NEW LANDS BUT SEEING WITH NEW EYES."
Marcel Proust

59

It's easy to be attentive when exploring the unknown. But, the familiar holds mystery and wonder, as well. View each new day as unexplored territory.

GIVE IN TO JOY

There's a little girl in you who understands the power of pure delight. Forget what others may think. Smile, giggle, praise, dance and clap your hands with glee. When you look for joy, you find it.

60

THE WORLD'S A GLORIOUS GALLERY

Look at the natural world...from the changing tides to the setting sun, wildflowers to wildebeests; you're surrounded by incomparable works of art. Do your part in caring for the world around you as you would any other priceless masterpiece.

61

IT'S OKAY NOT TO KNOW IT ALL

Unanswered questions are a part of life, particularly in the area of faith. Don't let what you don't know keep you on the sidelines. Act on what you understand and trust that God holds the answers for the rest.

62

HONESTLY WEIGH WHAT OTHERS SAY

63 Both compliments and criticism can be useful. Consider each prayerfully so you can discern any truth you need to hear. Hold onto what helps and let go of the rest.

MAKE FRIENDS
WITH THE PRODUCE SECTION

64 Fruits and veggies help keep your body looking and feeling great. They're also a "guilt free" snack. So, eat up! Delight in nature's sweet treat to you.

FIND PEACE
WITH YOUR IMPERFECTION

65 Giving your all in everything you do is an admirable trait. Expecting perfection is something else—impossible. Refuse to mentally beat yourself up when things don't go as planned. Say, "I forgive you" to yourself and mean it.

PAJAMA PARTIES
ARE NOT JUST FOR KIDS

Treat yourself to a night in. Turn off the
cell phone. Power down the computer. Take a
bubble bath. Enjoy a cup of tea. Start a book
you've wanted to read. Give yourself the gift of
relaxation in thanks for the hard work you've
put in today.

66

"TREAT YOUR FRIENDS AS YOU DO
YOUR PICTURES AND PLACE THEM
IN THEIR BEST LIGHT."
Jennie Jerome Churchill

67

Look for the best in the ones you love. Focus
on their strengths and extend grace for their
faults. Love them as you wish to be loved.

LIGHTEN YOUR LOAD

68

Combat the chaos of clutter. Tackle one drawer, one closet or corner of your home that could use a little extra TLC. Toss, organize and donate. The more in control your surroundings are, the more in control you'll feel about your life.

GET DOWN LIKE A PRO

69

Relearn the power of play by getting down on the floor with a child. Build a block fortress. Share a story. Tickle tiny toes. Dare to pretend. Enjoy the freedom of making up the rules as you go.

YOU HAVE THE POWER
TO MAKE SOMEONE'S DAY

70

Whether it's a word of encouragement, an impromptu hug or a quick text that reads, "I'm so glad you're my friend," you can lift someone's spirits in less than a minute. Whose will it be today?

"WHO IS WISE? HE THAT LEARNS
FROM EVERYONE."
Benjamin Franklin

71

Every person you meet can teach you something you don't already know. Be an attentive
student to the life lessons all around you.

TAKE A WALK DOWN MEMORY LANE

72

Recall a few of the happiest moments of your
life. Consider what made them so extraordinary.
Thank God for the pleasure and privilege of
having them written into your life story.

GET TO KNOW YOUR HERO

What inspired those you admire to become
heroes, leaders and role models? Do a little
digging. If you're acquainted, ask questions. If
he or she is a famous person, read a biography.
Allow lessons they've learned help bring out the
hero in you.

73

"YOU MUST DO THE THING
YOU THINK YOU CANNOT DO."
Eleanor Roosevelt

74

Everyone has fears. Who knows when you'll come face-to-face with yours? Instead of dreading that day, prepare for it. Deal with what lies at the heart of your fear. With God's help, there's nothing you can't overcome.

A GOOD EXAMPLE
IS THE BEST TEACHER

75

What you do will always speak louder than what you say. Encourage your children, or your co-workers, toward positive change by practicing what you preach—and you won't have to preach at all.

JUST BECAUSE THE SHOE FITS,
YOU DON'T HAVE TO BUY IT

76

Being content with what you have is a wonderfully stress-free way to live. Cultivate the habit of shopping only when you need to, instead of heading to the mall to lift your spirits or pass the time.

BUILD UP
INSTEAD OF MELTING DOWN

77

If your temper starts to rise, choose to act, instead of react. Stop, breathe and thoughtfully choose what you're going to do next. Choose words and actions that promote peace over pride, and grace over getting even.

SOMETIMES THE TOUGHEST JOBS ARE THE MOST WORTHWHILE

78

Take parenting, for instance. Or how about working to overcome an addiction or master a difficult skill? Just because something is hard, doesn't mean it can't be done. Commitment, patience and diligence are your keys to success.

REPENT INSTEAD OF REGRET

79

The word "repent" literally means "to turn around." While regret keeps looking back, bemoaning decisions made, repentance chooses to change the future by turning toward a new, more positive direction. Which way are you headed?

> "THERE IS JUST ONE LIFE
> FOR EACH OF US: OUR OWN."
> *Euripides*

Comparing your body, talents, love life or lifestyle with anyone else's leads down one of two roads: pride or discontent. Neither direction is pretty. The more you focus on your own unique journey, the more beauty you'll discover along the way.

80

EMPTY A BACKWARD BUCKET LIST

Instead of focusing on what you want out of life, briefly consider what you'd like to rid yourself of. A quick temper? A sarcastic streak? An unhealthy habit? Take a positive step to remove a negative trait or influence in your life today.

81

YOU ARE RICH, REGARDLESS OF YOUR TAX BRACKET

82

True riches cannot be held in your hands. They reside in your mind and your heart. Treasures like friendship, joy, peace, hope, faith and love won't tarnish or lose value over time. They only increase in value.

MAKE FRIENDS WITH YOUR AGE

83

Age isn't a number. It's a collage of memories and experiences, a treasure trove of wisdom and relationships, an unpredictable adventure that you alone have the opportunity to explore. Welcome each new year with gratitude and anticipation.

CHOOSE YOUR WORDS
LIKE DIAMONDS

Words have the power to shine truth and beauty into the lives of others. Don't settle for flawed, inferior gems. Be picky. Take your time to think carefully and prayerfully about what you're going to put on display.

84

GIVE FIRST IMPRESSIONS
A SECOND CHANCE

It's easy to jump to conclusions about what you like or don't like. But there are some foods, experiences—and even people—that are an acquired taste. Give 'em another try. You have more to gain than to lose.

85

"SHE WHO BEGINS MANY THINGS FINISHES BUT A FEW."
Proverb

86

Starting a project is easy. Finishing takes perseverance. Count the cost before you begin. Then keep moving forward toward completion, even if it's only one small step at a time.

CONFIDENCE KNOWS WHAT IT'S TALKING ABOUT

87

Being a self-assured woman begins with being self-aware. Be honest about what you can and cannot do. But don't be afraid to test your limits. Tomorrow, you could be a little stronger, a little wiser, a littler braver than you are today.

ENJOY THE FREEDOM
OF FOLLOWING THE RULES

When other drivers follow traffic laws, you're free to drive safely down the highway. Wise, judicious rules don't hinder freedom. They allow it to flourish. Consider what rules, laws or principles guide you each day.

88

YOU DON'T HAVE TO BE
A STAR TO SHINE

Not every woman is gifted with perfect pitch, an artistic edge or technological genius. Prodigies and superstars are exceptions, not the norm. You don't have to be the best. Just DO your best.

89

90
SAY WHAT YOU MEAN
AND MEAN WHAT YOU SAY
Be a woman of your word. If you say you're going to do something, be diligent in following through. Earning another's trust is a treasure worth guarding.

91
BE YOUR OWN BEST FRIEND
Patience, kindness, generosity, forgiveness… you extend the very best to those you love. Love yourself in kind. You deserve a friend like you.

92
BECOME A GOALIE
FOR YOUR OWN TEAM
Have a goal? Write it down. Break down how you can reach it by listing bite-sized, achievable action steps. Track your progress. Success is just a goal away.

"HE THAT WATERETH
SHALL BE WATERED ALSO."
Proverbs 11:25

When you reach out to help others, you help
yourself at the same time. It lifts your spirits by
taking your mind off your own problems and
reminds you what a pleasure it is to give love
away without expecting anything in return.

93

TAP INTO THE JOY
OF AN ORDINARY DAY

Happiness is fleeting… Fortunes reverse.
Moods swing. Hormones rage. Circumstances
change. But joy—that inner well of gratitude
and delight—is a constant source of strength.
Draw on it often.

94

GIVE YOURSELF
SOME BREATHING ROOM

Henry David Thoreau wrote, "Simplify, simplify, simplify." His advice still holds true today.
What can you cut out, throw out, or opt out of
that will help your life flow more smoothly?

95

KISS TODAY GOOD-BYE

96 Before you go to sleep, officially put "today" to bed. Celebrate the blessings. Let go of the failures. Restructure any worries about tomorrow into prayers. You've done all you can with today. Give it, and yourself, a rest.

MANY HAPPY RETURNS CAN BE A WISE MOVE

97 Don't hide an impulsive purchase in your closet. Regardless of whether it was the sale price, peer pressure or hormones that led you to buy something you're having second thoughts about, return it. You'll purchase more shrewdly next time.

CHOOSE YOUR BATTLES LIKE YOUR SWIMSUITS…WISELY

98 There are some things worth fighting for, even dying for. Before you throw yourself into battle, whether it's with words, actions or resources—in parenting or on principle—weigh what's at stake. Make sure it's a struggle worth engaging in.

"SYMPATHY IS TWO HEARTS TUGGING AT ONE LOAD."
Charles Henry Parkhurst

99

Grief is a burden that's meant to be shared. Even if you can't find the right words, your presence, your touch and your prayers can lighten the load of another.

LIFE IS A MARATHON, SO PACE YOURSELF

100

After God created the world, He took a day off. Even with considerably less miraculous responsibilities, your body, mind and spirit still need a break. Take time regularly to relax, reflect and play.

MAKE A CHANGE WITH YOUR CHANGE

When your budget it tight, continue to practice generosity. Empty your purse of change every day. At the end of the year, donate what you've saved to help those in need.

101

102

URGENCY OFTEN MASQUERADES AS EMERGENCY

The more jam-packed your To Do List, the more frantic life feels. Schedule yourself some wiggle room. When interruptions or opportunities arise, you won't slide into panic mode.

103

TOGETHER IS BETTER

Teamwork takes cooperation and delegation. Do all you can with what you have to accomplish your own task, but graciously assist others as your time, energy and talents allow. View your team as a body, working toward mutual good health.

104

LIVE A HEALTHIER TODAY

Trade the elevator for the stairs. Choose fruit over fries. Dust off your bicycle. Pack a sandwich instead of heading to the drive-thru. Little choices today can add up to big benefits tomorrow.

"A MISTY MORNING DOESN'T SIGNIFY A CLOUDY DAY."
Traditional Proverb

When facing an uphill battle, things may not look good from where you stand. But what you see isn't a full picture of what the future holds. Hang in there. Change is in the air.

105

AN UNEXPRESSED THOUGHT CAN BE A GIFT

Not everything that pops into your head demands to be said. Sometimes what you choose not to say can be as much of a gift as what you do.

106

APPLAUD THE SUNSET

Twice a day, weather permitting, the sky becomes an artist's canvas. Savor sunrise and sunset. Offer thanks that they herald the promise of a brand new day, over and over again.

107

108

LOVE IS MORE THAN A FEELING

If you're feeling annoyed or indifferent toward those you love, continue to choose to do and say the loving thing. Your feelings will follow your actions.

109

LIFE'S A MISSION, NOT AN INTERMISSION

How you spend your time is how you spend your life. What matters most to you? Purposefully invest your time, and yourself, in it. Plan how to move forward, so time won't slip away like loose change.

110

STREAMLINE YOUR SOCIAL MEDIA

Is Facebook, Twitter or texting adding or detracting from your day? Be as intentional about the words you send, as well as those you say.

MAKE NEW MISTAKES TOMORROW

No one gets it perfect every time, regardless of what "it" is. When you blow it, learn from it. There's no value in making the same mistake again.

111

SHARE YOUR GREATNESS

What do you excel at? Share it. Offer your experience and expertise by mentoring others. Encouraging them to succeed will make your own success even sweeter.

112

"IF THE WORLD SEEMS COLD TO YOU, KINDLE FIRES TO WARM IT."
Lucy Larcom

Some days are just plain tough. Take one step, no matter how small, to make it brighter for yourself or others.

113

RESISTANCE HELPS KEEP
A PLANE ALOFT

114

It's the struggle you face in accomplishing something worthwhile that often strengthens you to the point where you can succeed. Running against the wind has its benefits.

A GOOD CRY REALLY CAN BE GOOD

115

When your emotions are raw, find a safe space to let everything go. Release what you've been bottling up. Cry 'til you're dry. Then, pray. Compose your thoughts (on paper, if that helps). Get up, get out and begin again.

EVERY FRIEND IS A
DISTINCTIVE GEM

116

Every individual holds a singular sparkle. That's why friends defy comparison. Celebrate, and appreciate, each one for the incomparable beauty they bring to your life.

CHANGE THE CHANNEL

Your thoughts are the soundtrack of your life. If you don't like the tune, change it. Focus on the positive. Expose any lies you've believed about yourself for what they are. Revel in the truth.

117

"DREAMS ARE THE TOUCHSTONES OF OUR CHARACTER."
Henry David Thoreau

Are your deepest prayers and fondest dreams worthy of how much they require of your heart? What you long for reveals what you treasure most. Refuse to pine for fool's gold.

118

GETTING READY IS PART OF SUCCESS

The time you invest in mastering a skill, raising money, overcoming roadblocks and even making mistakes can all be steps forward, even if they feel like running in place. The big picture is much larger than you can see.

119

WITH SACRIFICE, LESS IS MORE

120

When you put your comfort, resources, time and love on the line to benefit another, you'll find your ability and desire to give grows right along with your own gratitude. It's win-win all around.

COME OUT OF HIDING

121

Do you wield a shield throughout the day? Do you use humor, silence, busyness or even what you wear to hide the true you? You're an original. A one-of-a-kind masterpiece. A copy is never as amazing as the real thing. Olly olly oxen free!

IMAGINE THE POSSIBLE

122

A mountain that looks impossible to climb may be easily conquered when approached from the opposite side. When a problem has you stumped, let your imagination run free. A different point of view just might hold the key you need.

PEACE IS AN INSIDE JOB

Peace of mind can coexist in chaotic circumstances. Lean on faith, hope and love as your constant eye in any storm. Do what you can right now, even if all you can do is pray.

123

"BE KIND, FOR EVERYONE YOU MEET IS FIGHTING A HARD BATTLE."
Philo Judaeus

The driver who cuts you off, the clerk who snaps at you, the friend who doesn't even say "hello"…it's easy to make a snap judgment about others. But you never know what's going on behind the scenes. The "benefit of the doubt" is a gracious gift.

124

YOU'RE A POWERFUL WOMAN

125

Through your words, your actions and your love, you have the power to change history. Whether you impact one life or many, you can make a positive difference in the world. That's no small thing.

MAKE NICE ON THE PLAYGROUND AND SHARE

126

You've worked hard for what you have. But it's also a gift. Every opportunity you've received isn't guaranteed. It's grace. So, hold loosely to what you have. Discover the joy of sharing what you've received.

A WISDOM BREAK PREVENTS MISTAKES

127

"Intelligence" knows things. "Wisdom" knows what to do with what you know. When you take a moment to think before you act you can turn a smart move, into a wise one.

"GREAT NECESSITIES CALL FORTH GREAT LEADERS."
Abigail Adams

Whether you feel like a natural-born leader or not, sometimes you just need to step up and get in the game. Do what you can about what you care about and others will follow.

128

LET OTHERS PRAISE YOUR SUCCESS

Knowing you've done a good job is one thing. Making sure everyone else knows it is quite another. Allow others the pleasure of tooting your horn. It makes for a more pleasant melody all around.

129

KEEP YOUR DANCE CARD OPEN

Time's too short to be the kind of friend you'd like to be with everyone you meet. But don't let that stop you from adding to your circle of friends. A new friend may become the old friend you celebrate years from now.

130

BECOME A WAIT WATCHER

131

Patience isn't a passive pursuit. While you're waiting, keep watching. Signs of change or answers to prayer may be all around you. They're simply more difficult to see if you're focused on something else.

TRUTH COMES IN ONLY ONE SIZE

132

Truth can't be stretched. What is…is. Period. Getting in the habit of telling the truth, without any embellishment from little white lies, assures those around you that they can trust your words— and your character.

THE BENEFITS OF BEING "UNDER THE INFLUENCE"

133

Part of growing up is learning from those who are older, and wiser, than yourself. You're still growing. Seek out older women you admire. Ask questions. Listen carefully. Allow them to influence you in wonderful ways.

FIGHT ON YOUR KNEES

When you get to the point where you've done all you can, there's still one more thing you can do. Pray. Some battles are simply too big for you to win on your own.

134

GET COZY WITH A DIFFERENT CULTURE

The world's a crazy quilt of customs, languages and beliefs. Reach out around the globe—or right next door. Read a book. Watch a film. Try a new recipe. Better yet, make a new friend who can help you see the world through her eyes.

135

GENTLENESS IS A SIGN OF STRENGTH

Restraint is what makes strength useful, instead of destructive. If you need to deliver a difficult message to a friend or a lesson on obedience to a child, let gentleness temper your words and actions.

136

137

"AS THE PURSE IS EMPTIED
THE HEART IS FILLED."
Victor Hugo

Hugo wasn't promoting a spending spree.
He was talking about investing both your love
and your resources in the lives of others. Fill
your heart with what can't be lost, stolen or
taken away.

138

CIRCLE THE WAGONS OF FRIENDSHIP

Friendship is more than sharing coffee or a
movie together. It's celebrating each other's
triumphs, grieving each other's losses and
helping each other stand strong when times
are tough. There's no sweeter place to be than
"there" for one another.

139

EVERY ACTION BEGINS
WITH A THOUGHT

Stop and help… Call a friend… Go ahead
and volunteer… Speak up… Before casting off
a fleeting thought, weigh it. What sounds like
a random notion may be an opportunity for
growth and grace.

"A MOTHER IS NOT A PERSON TO
LEAN ON, BUT A PERSON TO MAKE
LEANING UNNECESSARY."
Dorothy Canfield Fisher

140

If you have the privilege of mothering a
child, do so with an eye toward the future.
Allow your children to experience, and learn
from, the consequences of their own actions.

EVERYTHING YOU DO
IS A SELF-PORTRAIT

Every job you tackle, every word you speak,
every gift you give paints a picture of who you
are. Let the true you shine through in all you do
by autographing your work with excellence.

141

COUNTING THE COST
IS A WISE INVESTMENT

142

Before committing to spend your time, money or energy in a big way, stop and consider the big picture. Weigh the true toll, including the potential emotional one. Don't spend more than you have—of anything.

TAKE YOURSELF LIGHTLY

143

Being able to laugh at yourself—without believing you're a joke—is a delicate balancing act. But it's one worth mastering. Give up trying to impress others and simply enjoy being you. It's one key to a "lighter" life.

THE GRASS ISN'T GREENER,
IT JUST LOOKS THAT WAY
FROM A DISTANCE

Every woman has an inside story, the real life she lives behind closed doors. Cast off assumptions gleaned from outward appearances. Understand others better by getting to know them for who they really are.

144

"COMMUNITY IS THE PLACE
WHERE GOD COMPLETES
OUR LIVES WITH HIS JOY."
Henri Nouwen

You were created to love and be loved. Whether it's your friends, family, neighbors or church, those close to you not only help shape your life, but who you are.

145

WIGGLE WHILE YOU WORK

146

You don't have to work harder to work smarter. Take a quick break every hour. Walk around. Wiggle your fingers. Swing your arms. Kick up your heels. (In the bathroom, if need be!) Your brain and body will thank you for it!

RECONSIDER WHAT'S FOR DESSERT

147

A treat is whatever's sweet to you. Consider what you truly enjoy…bubble baths, reading, organizing, chatting with friends, nibbling beef jerky. When you need a pick-me-up, treat yourself in a way that best suits you.

EXPAND YOUR PERIPHERAL VISION

Want to help but are unsure of where to start? Start by paying attention. Both friends and strangers are full of clues, visual and verbal, as to how they're really doing. Pray for the ability to see, and act, on what others might miss.

148

THE MORE RARE,
THE MORE VALUABLE

You may accept that endangered animals, long-lost masterpieces or gargantuan gemstones are rare, and therefore both precious and valuable. But consider the fact there's only ONE of you. Precious, valuable, exquisitely made… that's you.

149

WINTER IS WHAT HELPS
MAKE SPRING SO SWEET

150

It's easy to take for granted what you enjoy all the time. It's the restless nights, the missed meals or bouts with illness that remind you what a joy daily blessings like sleep, food and health can be.

FRUIT RIPENS WHEN IT'S READY

151

Microwaves, credit cards, text messages… instant is pretty much the expected speed limit for today's society. Nature's a more realistic teacher. Learn from the seasons. Patience yields sweet fruit in the orchard and in life.

"IT IS NEVER TOO LATE TO BE WHAT YOU MIGHT HAVE BEEN."
George Eliot

152

Life's too brief to do everything you desire. But every minute affords a fresh opportunity to grow—to become a better friend, mother, neighbor…woman. Let love guide the way.

BELIEVE THOSE WHO KNOW YOU BEST

153

When you're feeling self-critical, pull out any cards or thank you notes you've saved. (If you don't save them, start.) Read, and re-read, what those who love you have to say about you. Take this truth to heart.

CHANGE YOUR ATTITUDE; CHANGE YOUR LIFE

154

Changing your job, your hair or your address may give you a temporary boost. If you're looking for long-lasting change, try your attitude. The way you view life directly influences how much you enjoy it.

"HAPPINESS IS A BUTTERFLY WHICH, WHEN PURSUED, IS ALWAYS BEYOND OUR GRASP, BUT, IF YOU WILL SIT DOWN QUIETLY, MAY ALIGHT UPON YOU."
Nathaniel Hawthorne

155

Slow down and sit awhile. Look at the beauty around you. Joy is close at hand.

TAKE THE PLUNGE

156

Don't allow your fear of wearing a swimsuit in public keep you on the sidelines. Hold your head up and dive on in. Everyone else is just as self-conscious as you.

DELIGHT IN THE DETOURS

When your day heads a different direction than you planned, don't miss the scenery along the way. Keep your eyes and heart open for unexpected opportunities, beauty and blessings. "Off track" may be exactly where you need to be.

157

NAPS AREN'T JUST FOR KIDS

Sometimes the best pick-me-up is to lay your self down. Just a fifteen or twenty minute nap can revive you physically and mentally. Give yourself two fresh starts today by getting out of bed twice.

158

"ONLY THE MEDIOCRE ARE ALWAYS AT THEIR BEST."
Jean Giraudoux

Down days happen. You blow it. You're moody and selfish. You're off your game. Put it behind you. Apologize and move on. Every moment of time offers a fresh opportunity to turn things around.

159

WEIGH WHO'S LEADING THE WAY

160

Choose carefully whose example and advice you follow. Only those who are worthy of your love, respect and admiration will lead you down a path worth traveling.

HONOR YOUR ANGELS

161

Not all angels have wings. But they can certainly be an answer to prayer. Anytime someone blesses your life, voice your appreciation…then pay that kindness forward by being an angel in someone else's life.

CELEBRATE THE WONDERS OF WOMANHOOD

162

Being a woman opens your life to unique blessings and challenges. Celebrate them both. Enjoy what's fantastic about femininity. Accept challenges as an inspiration to push you beyond perceived boundaries toward new frontiers.

A FULL LIFE ISN'T SYNONYMOUS WITH A FULL SCHEDULE

Ultimately, it's people—not promotions or possessions—that make a life truly fulfilling. If you're too busy to build stronger relationships, you're too busy.

163

"IT IS THE WOUNDED OYSTER THAT MENDS ITS SHELL WITH PEARL."
Ralph Waldo Emerson

Tough times can expose inner beauty. Strength, compassion, generosity, selflessness… allow difficulties to make you better, instead of bitter.

164

MOVE IT OR LOSE IT

If you're motivation is lagging, consider what's at stake. Really. Make a list of the reasons why you're doing what you're doing. Keeping those in mind can help get you moving—or inspire you to change direction.

165

"ANONYMOUS"
CAN DO GREAT THINGS

166

A toddler's motto is "Look at me! Look at me!" Grown women know the privilege of working behind the scenes. You don't have to be in the spotlight to make a difference.

LEARN TO RECOGNIZE
A GOOD WHINE

167

A "good whine" can flow easily when you're persevering through tough times. But it doesn't help you or those around you. Listen for it. If you've said it more than once, stop the flow. Transform it into a prayer or a challenge for change.

"FRIENDSHIP DOUBLES OUR JOYS
AND DIVIDES OUR GRIEF."
Proverb

168

A good friend knows what to do with both good news and bad news. Share yours freely. Ask about others' frequently, listening patiently and prayerfully.

EAT THE CUPCAKE

There's a time to treat yourself! Do the unexpected. Dance like no one's looking. Sing as though you're a natural-born diva. Plan that vacation. Take a break and rejuvenate!

169

WALK AWAY FROM THE CUPCAKE

There are times when it's best to "just say 'no.'" Leading a balanced life means making wise choices. Although what's necessary isn't always necessarily fun, it's wise. It ultimately leads to a happier, healthier life.

170

"THE MOST POWERFUL WEAPON ON EARTH IS THE HUMAN SOUL ON FIRE."
Ferdinand Foch

What you care about, you care for. If there's a cause that sets your blood boiling, put that heat to good use. Join others in making the change in the world you want to see.

171

HANG ONTO HOPE

172

You can be an optimist and a realist. There's always hope. Tough times don't last forever. Miracles do happen. Even when circumstances don't seem to change, you can. Do all you can to bring the "best" out of even the worst situation.

HANDLE OTHERS WITH CARE

173

Every person you meet is like a priceless piece of pottery: precious and fragile. Not every person lives up to what they're worth. But, you can. Be kind and gentle with how you handle others, friends and strangers alike.

COMPLIMENTS ARE BEST SERVED LIKE CASSEROLES...WARM

174

If you like a woman's shoes...tell her. The same goes for anything else she does or is. Let compliments flow easily from your lips. You know how good it feels to receive them.

LOVE IS A VERB

Saying "I love you" is important. But without loving actions, those words are simply sweet sentiments. What's one thing you can do today to show those you love how you feel without saying a word?

175

SEPARATE YOUR MOUNTAINS
FROM YOUR MOLEHILLS

Not all bumps in the road are created equal. When you face an obstacle, evaluate it before tackling it. Devote the time, effort and emotional energy each problem warrants. No more, no less.

176

"WRITE INJURIES IN SAND,
KINDNESSES IN MARBLE."
Proverb

Both pardon and appreciation are within your power to give. Offer them generously, regardless if you receive in return what you've bestowed.

177

JUST ONE MORE

178

When you hit a wall, turn "I can't" into "Just one more." Put all your energy into pushing yourself just a bit beyond what you think you can do. Tomorrow, push yourself one step farther. Little by little you can go far.

YOU DON'T HAVE TO FIX EVERYTHING THAT'S BROKEN

179

When a friend shares a problem, ask if she'd like your advice before offering it. She may just need to express how she's feeling aloud. Listening is doing something.

DRESS YOURSELF FROM THE INSIDE-OUT

180

Clothes don't "make the woman." They don't have that kind of power. Who you are, not what you wear, is your true source of beauty. Check your heart, as well as the mirror, each morning.

SPEND AN EVENING WITH THE STARS

Not all the stars are dancing on TV. Some are orbiting right above your head. Look up and marvel. Consider the mysteries yet to be solved, the frontiers left to explore.

181

"THOUGHT IS ACTION IN REHEARSAL."
Sigmund Freud

Good intentions can only take you so far. Without action, they're nothing more than random thoughts. Step up. Transform your best intentions into reality.

182

PUSH RIGHT PAST THE FINISH LINE

When runners see the finish line, they don't slow down because the end's in sight. They give everything they've got left to reach it. Follow their lead with every job you do.

183

GIVE YOUR HEART A HEAD START

184 You never know for sure where today is going to take you. Before you hop out of bed, prepare for the best. Take five minutes to bring to mind things you're thankful for. It will help set the tone for the rest of the day.

"YOU CAN'T CARRY TWO FACES UNDER ONE HAT."
Proverb

185 At the store, in the car, at church, at work or at home, there's only one person you need to be…yourself. Relax and let the true you show through, with friends and strangers alike.

LEARN THE SKILL OF SITTING STILL

186 Doing nothing isn't always doing nothing. Sit quietly in a public place. Listen. Observe. Enjoy the sun or wind on your face. See what you can discover that you would otherwise have missed.

CHANGE YOUR STATUS QUO

Challenge yourself. Whether it's running a marathon or just around the block, don't accept who you are today as who you'll be tomorrow. Learn. Risk. Try. Go ahead and grow!

187

WAKE YOURSELF UP

More than once a day, if necessary. Become more attentive to what you say and do, as well as the beauty of the world around you. Reawaken yourself to be fully present in the present.

188

SHAKE HANDS WITH
THE STRANGER INSIDE

Certain weaknesses only surface under stress, anger or pain. Acknowledge they're part of who you really are. Don't excuse them. Deal with them. Bad habits are always worth breaking, even if they're visible only to you.

189

MAKE A PLAYDATE

190

Regardless of what age or stage of life you're in, you never outgrow the need to play. Board game, basketball, a jigsaw puzzle, video game… whatever you choose to do, set your care aside and enjoy.

"IN PRAYER IT IS BETTER TO HAVE A HEART WITHOUT WORDS THAN WORDS WITHOUT A HEART."

John Bunyan

191

There's no secret formula for prayer. No magic words or perfect position. All it takes is a humble heart. Share what's there. The rest is in God's hands.

"MAÑANA IS THE BUSIEST DAY
OF THE WEEK."
Proverb
"Some day" usually translates to "never," if
you don't get it on the calendar. Set a due date
for anything you tend to procrastinate doing.

192

"A KIND HEART IS A FOUNTAIN OF
GLADNESS, MAKING EVERYTHING IN
ITS VICINITY FRESHEN INTO SMILES."
Washington Irving
When you're kind to others, others act in
kind. Inspire a wake of joy to flow through
today by showing how much you care in a
tangible way.

193

GO GROCERY SHOPPING
ON YOUR OWN SHELVES

194

Kitchen shelves need cleaning? Try a one-week grocery moratorium. Toss any product that's expired. List what's left. Make your menus from that list, with minimal purchases. Have fun saving money and wasting less food.

WHEN YOU'RE FEELING LONELY,
YOU'RE NOT ALONE

195

Others feel exactly the same way. Do yourself, and them, a favor. Reach out. Make brownies for your neighbors. Invite a widow or single mom over. Call a friend. Don't wait for someone to call you. Make the first move.

FRIENDSHIP IS THE
ULTIMATE MAKEOVER

The more you love someone, the more attractive they become in your eyes. Spend time getting to know, and love, your friends even more than you do. You'll all grow more beautiful!

196

INTIMACY REQUIRES HONESTY

A true friend not only accepts, but embraces, the true you. But she can't embrace what she doesn't know is there. Risk revealing your insecurities, past failures and fears. The less there is between you, the closer you can become.

197

BECOME A PICK UP ARTIST

198

Clean up after yourself. Whether it's dirty dishes in the kitchen or careless words that messed up a relationship. The sooner you take care of a mess, the simpler it is to clean.

"DON'T JUDGE EACH DAY BY THE HARVEST YOU REAP BUT BY THE SEEDS YOU PLANT."
Robert Louis Stevenson

199

Every little thing you do for others matters. You may never know how much. Make today count in lots of wonderful ways!

"ONE DAY IN PERFECT HEALTH IS MUCH."
Proverb

If you're feeling good today, be thankful. If you're ill or injured, celebrate what's working well and the human body's remarkable ability to heal. Either way, make healthy choices a part of your daily routine.

200

A BOGGLED MIND EQUALS A HUMBLED HEART

Not everything in life can be explained through science and the laws of nature. Celebrate the amazing, extraordinary, unexpected and divine. Your heart can embrace what your mind can't fully understand or explain.

201

FLEXIBILITY IS GOOD FOR MORE THAN JUST YOGA

202

When life throws you a curve…flex. Instead of holding tightly to what was, throw yourself fully into what is. Better to bend than break.

TREAT MONEY FOR WHAT IT IS

203

Money is a tool, like a hammer, a vacuum or a blow dryer. You use it to help you accomplish a task. Don't build a relationship with it. Use it to build good things into your life and the lives of others.

HEROES ARE REVEALED, NOT MADE

204

You don't need superhuman strength to be a hero, only strength of character. Under pressure, the true you will show through, allowing your heart of gold the chance to shine.

BE CHOOSEY

Facing a big decision? Don't face it alone. Advice, common sense and experience are all wise counselors. Consult them before giving a final answer.

205

"IT OFTEN REQUIRES MORE COURAGE TO DARE TO DO RIGHT THAN TO FEAR TO DO WRONG."
Abraham Lincoln

Don't let pressure from others override your conscience. Do the right thing. The choice is yours. Make your choice count.

206

RAISE YOUR HAND

You're an intelligent woman. But you can't possibly know it all. Asking questions shows you're wise, as well as smart. You're open to learning something new.

207

LEARN FROM YOUR LIFE

208

Set your memory on rerun. Pinpoint defining moments in your life. What's brought you to where you are today? Celebrate how far you've come.

"BY CRAWLING A CHILD LEARNS TO STAND."
Proverb

209

Being good at anything begins with baby steps—and includes a few tumbles along the way. Keep going. It's the only way to master what you've got in mind.

FLATTER YOURSELF

210

Assess your wardrobe. If it's worn out, doesn't fit, out of style or you just never wear it—get rid of it. Having fewer, better choices makes getting ready less stressful.

AWARD YOURSELF A BONUS

Mentally list all those little unpaid jobs you do everyday (cooking, cleaning, carpooling, etc.). Recognize how many hours you really put in. Treat yourself to a "Let It Slide Day." You've earned it.

211

RESPECT YOUR ELDERS
BY REMINISCING

You've heard older friends and relatives share the same stories a thousand times. Go for 1001. Honor them by asking questions about their past. Listen and learn.

212

"NO ONE CAN MAKE YOU FEEL INFERIOR WITHOUT YOUR CONSENT."
Eleanor Roosevelt

There's no cookie cutter for the "perfect" you. You're in the process of "becoming"… one word, one action, one day at a time. Only you can say how far you've come or have to go.

213

MOVE AT THE SPEED OF LIFE, INSTEAD OF LIGHT

214

Focused and efficient is better than fast and sloppy. You only want to do a job once, so take the time you need to do it right.

"HOLD A TRUE FRIEND WITH BOTH HANDS."
Proverb

215

It's easy to take low maintenance friends for granted, especially those you've known "forever." But there is no "forever" friendship. Hold them close now.

ELIMINATE EXCUSES

216

Trying to "save face" by weaving a tale of woe doesn't fool anyone—and it's beneath a wonderful woman like you. When things go wrong, own up to it. Apologize, make things right and move on.

ON THE SIDELINES IS AN IMPORTANT PLACE TO BE

When you encourage others, you play a role in their success. Keep cheering. Your words may be the ones that help a friend persevere past the finish line.

217

"BE NOT WATER, TAKING THE TINT OF ALL COLORS."
Proverb

Protection, acceptance, insecurity…women choose to blend in with the crowd for many reasons. But you're not a chameleon. You're a singular sensation. Stand up and stand out!

218

LORD, MAY I BE DIRECTED WHAT TO DO AND WHAT TO LEAVE UNDONE.
Elizabeth Fry

Every day is a juggling act. Instead of letting balls fall, choose which ones to take out of the mix today and then toss back in tomorrow.

219

220

"I AM A LITTLE PENCIL IN THE HAND
OF A WRITING GOD WHO IS SENDING
A LOVE LETTER TO THE WORLD."
Mother Teresa

Your legacy is written one day at a time. What
kind of "letter" will you write today?

221

NO MAN—OR WOMAN—IS AN ISLAND

Consider how many people it takes to
provide you with a loaf of bread. Farmers,
bakers, packagers, grocers…even the folks who
assembled your car help get that bread home.
We need each other. Appreciate being part of a
worldwide team.

222

GOOD FRIENDS
ARE EXCELLENT EDITORS

Sharing everything with your friends doesn't
really mean "everything." A good friend knows
when it's time to say, "And what's new with you?"

WE'RE ALL RUNNING THE SAME RACE

Regardless of what we look like—the color of our hair or skin, the labels on our clothes or stage of life we're in—we're all members of the same race. The human race. Let's run side-by-side, getting to know each other from the inside out.

223

"VISION IS THE ART OF SEEING THE INVISIBLE."
Jonathan Swift

To look beyond today to what might be someday takes inspiration and imagination. Think big. Then share your vision. You're one step closer to seeing a dream come true.

224

THIS TOO SHALL PASS…

Hold tightly to these four words. They'll help you hold tightly to true perspective. Everything comes to an end, both good and bad. Savor or persevere, whatever today requires.

225

226

"DON'T BE AFRAID TO TAKE A BIG
STEP. YOU CAN'T CROSS A CHASM
IN TWO SMALL JUMPS."
David Lloyd George

Whether it's personally, professionally,
financially or spiritually, when your gut says
you've got to take a leap of faith, listen. Weigh
the risk. Get advice. Pray. Leap…

227

YOU HAVE A GIFT FOR
LOVING OTHERS WELL

Your circle of friends is a reflection of the
beauty found in your own heart. Be thankful
for your friends, but know your own gift of
love has helped draw them into your life.

228

TO FOLLOW YOUR BLISS
YOU'VE GOT TO FIND IT

There's plenty you need to do. But what do you
love to do? Figure out what you're truly passionate
about. From painting a masterpiece to supporting
a cause, find time to do what energizes you.

THERE ARE SEEDS
OF GREATNESS IN YOU

Your abilities, strengths, desires and dreams all hold marvelous potential. Cultivate them with purpose and perseverance. When the season's right, you'll harvest success.

229

"IT'S NOT HOW OLD YOU ARE,
BUT HOW YOU ARE OLD."
Marie Dressler

As you age, inhibitions drop by the wayside. In other words, you become more of who you really are. Nurturing kind, generous ways today is the best beauty treatment for tomorrow.

230

DESTROY YOUR ENEMIES
BY MAKING THEM FRIENDS

You don't have to draw close to those you don't trust. But you can pray for God's best in their lives. Regardless of whether your "enemies" change, your heart will—and so will the way you look at them.

231

"COURAGE IS FEAR
THAT HAS SAID ITS PRAYERS."
Dorothy Bernard

232

It's doing what needs to be done in the face
of resistance, even when you're afraid. Be bold.
Be brave. Face what you fear and do what you
know needs to be done.

PAIN IS YOUR WARNING LIGHT

233

Pain has a purpose. It lets you know something's wrong. Don't ignore it or medicate it
before you investigate it. Thank God for the
warning. Then, heed it.

"THE MORE POSSESSIONS
THE MORE WORRY."
Hillel

234

The more you have, the more you have to care
for—and to lose. Consider the full cost of each
purchase, not just to your budget, but to your
time and heart, as well.

EYE-TO-EYE INVITES
HEART-TO-HEART

Looking others in the eye can be uncomfortable because it makes you feel exposed, vulnerable…"seen." But it's also a great way to make a compassionate connection. Give others your full attention. Open your heart, as well as your eyes.

235

JOY CAFFEINATES YOUR LIFE

Feel like you're running on empty? Reach for a jolt of joy instead a cup of joe. Step out into the sunshine. Call a friend. Arrange a bouquet of flowers. Thank God for the people in your life. Joy is within reach.

236

"SEARCH THY OWN HEART;
WHAT PAINETH THEE IN OTHERS
IN THYSELF MAY BE."
John Greenleaf Whittier

What drives you nuts? Next time you're annoyed with someone, ask yourself why. What does your frustration reveal about you?

237

LET THEM KNOW

238

You have people in your life who mean the world to you. Just hearing their name, or catching sight of their smile, makes your heart warm. Warm their hearts with your words of love and appreciation today.

PREVENT IDENTITY THEFT

239

Anytime you try and act like someone you're not, the true you is forced into hiding. Nothing that rare and irreplaceable deserves to live in the shadows. Come on out. Genuine outshines imitation every time.

"YOU WILL BREAK THE BOW IF YOU KEEP IT ALWAYS BENT."
Proverb

240

You are resilient. You can bounce back from a few sleepless nights, skipped meals or nights of overtime. But if the exception becomes your new normal, you'll no longer have as much to give. Take a break...so you won't.

TEST YOUR PLUMBLINE

A building is said to have "integrity" when it's structurally solid. The same is true of people. A life built on a foundation of faith, love and authenticity can't be shaken.

241

"JUST A LITTLE MORE" IS NEVER ENOUGH

Discontent is like an itch that can never be scratched long enough. Choose to enjoy what you have right now, instead of longing for the next big thing. The race for just a little more is one with no finish line.

242

FREE THE DANCER IN YOU

You don't need to know any fancy steps to move to the music—even if the music is only playing inside you. Cast off your inhibitions and move. Hop, skip, jump and jive. Your body needs some playtime.

243

244

"A TIME TO GET, AND A TIME
TO LOSE; A TIME TO KEEP,
AND A TIME TO CAST AWAY."
Ecclesiastes 3:6

What time is it for you? All life flows in cycles
and seasons. What worked for you yesterday
may need revised or tossed today. When change
beckons, go with the flow.

245

SAVOR SIMPLE PLEASURES

A cup of tea, unexpectedly seeing a friend, a
favorite song played on the radio…what little
gifts will grace today? Embrace each one with a
thankful heart.

246

"IT'S EASY TO HALVE THE POTATOES
WHERE THERE'S LOVE."
Proverb

Less feels like more when you share it with
those you love. Consider the sacrifices others
have made for you, big and small—and rest in
knowing how deeply you're loved.

THERE'S NO NEED TO OUTSOURCE YOUR INSIGHT

Women's intuition is more than a gut feeling. It's your wisdom, experience and perception all working in sync to send you a message. Listen to it. Weigh it against common sense. Pray about it. Then, act on it.

247

YOUR WORST ENEMY OR BEST FRIEND MAY BE YOURSELF

Are you for—or against—yourself? You have enough battles to fight in this life without knocking yourself down. Speak kindly to everyone, including you.

248

"READING IS TO THE MIND WHAT EXERCISE IS TO THE BODY."
Joseph Addison

A good book is like a personal trainer for your mind. Give your imagination a workout. Stretch your vocabulary. Strengthen your focus. Switch off the TV and switch on your mind.

249

IMAGINATION AND MEMORY OFTEN DANCE TOGETHER

250

Memory isn't a reliable reporter. Time, or strong emotion, can twist facts toward fiction. Always leave room for the chance that what you think happened may not have happened exactly as you think.

YOU CAN GROW SEPARATELY WITHOUT GROWING APART

251

Whether it's your best friend, your children or your spouse, sharing life together is an immeasurable joy. But ultimately, every person has his or her own life to live. Hold each other close. Just make sure you each have room to breathe.

"BEST FRIEND, MY WELL-SPRING IN THE WILDERNESS!"
George Eliot

252

A best friend is the precious gem on the golden band of your circle of friends. Get to know every facet of her character. Celebrate how she adds sparkle to your life.

WELCOME WONDER AND AWE

What if today you experienced life for the very first time? In some ways, you do. Each day is a new creation. For a fresh, joy-filled perspective approach today with childlike wonder and curiosity.

253

"THERE'S NO PILLOW SO SOFT AS A CLEAR CONSCIENCE."

Proverb

Do your part to right a wrong the first chance you get. You'll sleep, breathe and smile so much easier.

254

INVEST WISELY

Make a deposit into the memory banks of those you love. Surprise them. Honor them. Inspire tears of laughter or joy. Sincere expressions of affection continue to accrue interest as favorite memories are revisited again and again.

255

YOU KNOW MORE THAN
YOU THINK YOU DO

256

Second guessing your decisions can leave you frustrated, confused and headed nowhere. Trust yourself. Your first response is usually your best.

FRIENDS ARE THE BEST DÉCOR

257

The key to hospitality isn't fancy furniture, gourmet meals or a perfectly organized spice rack. It's love. Open your heart when you open your door and every guest will feel right at home.

"I PRAY THEE O GOD,
THAT I MAY BE BEAUTIFUL WITHIN."
Socrates

258

Beauty isn't only skin deep. True beauty shines from the inside out. The best beauty regime is one that addresses what lasts longest and matters most.

YOU CAN'T PLEASE EVERYBODY

You're a true treasure. But not everyone will treasure you. That doesn't mean there's anything wrong with you. Some people just won't get you. Don't let it get to you.

259

EXCELLENCE IS A MOVING TARGET

A toddler and an adult may both do an excellent job at a given task. But the results will be far from identical. Do your best today, understanding full well that tomorrow your best has the potential to be even better.

260

TRUE LOVE IS BEYOND MEASURE

A good relationship isn't a 50-50 proposition. It's two people giving 100% of themselves to each other. Be a friend others rejoice to know. Don't hold back what's within your power to give.

261

SWEEP THE SKELETONS
OUT OF YOUR CLOSET

262

No bones about it, secrets can eat away at your peace of mind. Bring them into the light. Share them with someone you trust. Once exposed, they're easier to dispose.

CHECK YOUR BEARINGS

263

Life can feel like you're racing at 100 mph. What if you're headed the wrong direction? Look at your life with a critical eye. Where do you want to be a year from now? Five years? Ten? Make sure the road you're on is headed there.

"IF I HAVE BEEN ABLE TO SEE
FARTHER THAN OTHERS,
IT IS BECAUSE I HAVE STOOD ON
THE SHOULDERS OF GIANTS."
Sir Isaac Newton

264

Your creative fire is partially fueled by the ideas and inventions of others. In turn, you may be the inspiration that moves future generations.

WABI-SABI ISN'T
A SUSHI RESTAURANT

The Japanese culture reveres the features of wabi-sabi. It's the beauty found in things that are imperfect, impermanent or incomplete. Seek to appreciate the wabi-sabi in you.

265

YOU'LL FIND WHAT
YOU'RE LOOKING FOR

If you're looking for the best in yourself and others, you'll find it. The same is true if you're looking for the worst. Which will it be? The choice is up to you.

266

VULNERABILITY ISN'T WEAKNESS

Being candid about your fears, failures and imperfections is a sign of strength. It shows you're comfortable in your own skin, yet willing to grow. It also encourages others to be more vulnerable in return.

267

268

"FAITH IS THE DARING OF THE SOUL
TO GO FARTHER THAN IT CAN SEE."
William Newton Clarke

Much of life's out of your control. That calls
for faith in something bigger than yourself.
With God's help you can handle what you
can't control.

269

NOT ALL SHORTCUTS
ARE CREATED EQUAL

What's expedient or convenient can be help-
ful. But speed and ease shouldn't outweigh
what's kind, honest or prudent. A decision is
judged both by its benefits and its cost.

"FEW THINGS HELP AN INDIVIDUAL
MORE THAN TO PLACE
RESPONSIBILITY UPON HIM AND LET
HIM KNOW THAT YOU TRUST HIM."

Booker T. Washington

Delegating tasks to others is both wise and
kind. Give others the chance to shine and grow.

270

YOUR BRAIN'S TOO
BRIGHT TO BE BORED

A lack of options isn't what leaves you feeling
lackluster. It's a lack of inspiration. Wake up
your enthusiasm by shaking up your routine. In
a world this big, there's always something new to
do or pursue.

271

272

> "THERE IS NO SUCH THING
> IN ANYONE'S LIFE
> AS AN UNIMPORTANT DAY."
>
> *Alexander Woollcott*

You matter. That means that what you do and say matters, as well. Every day is a new opportunity to live, learn and love. Seize it with open arms.

273

A LITTLE SILLINESS
IS GOOD FOR THE SOUL

Good friends bring out the kid in each other. The freedom to laugh with, and not at, one another is a stress-reliever and spirit-raiser at any age.

BE A LABEL REMOVER

Homeless, wealthy, divorced, addict, celebrity...
words like these describe situations people are in.
They don't tell you who they are. When a "label"
pops into your mind, refuse to let it stick. Focus
on the person underneath.

274

TIME IS A GIFT
THAT CAN'T BE RETURNED

When you give your time, you literally give
your life. The same is true of those who give
their time to you. Remembering what a priceless, irreplaceable gift time is helps you give, and
receive, it with intentionality and appreciation.

275

THE FIRST STEP IS A DOOZIE

276

You know that thing you've been putting off? The toughest part is taking the first step. Fears, expectations, self-doubt…they can distort your idea of what lies ahead. The only way to get a clear picture of reality is to begin.

TODAY'S THE YOUNGEST YOU'VE YET TO BE

277

Put your youth to good use—regardless of how old you are. Do what you can with what you've got, wherever today takes you.

LOVE CHANGES
THE FACE OF THE CROWD

Every friend was once a stranger. If you feel self-conscious or shy in a crowd, picture everyone around you as someone you already know and love. The more comfortable you feel, the easier it is for this fantasy to become reality.

278

"IF YOU CAN'T FEED A HUNDRED
PEOPLE, THEN JUST FEED ONE."
Mother Teresa

279

Do you have enough to eat today? If so, give thanks. Then go a step farther. Share the blessing. You can help change the world one life at a time.

"BUYING ON CREDIT IS ROBBING NEXT YEAR'S CROP."

Proverb

280

Enjoy the freedom of living within your means. The less you owe, the freer you are to take advantage of unexpected opportunities that come your way.

CHANGE IS HERE TO STAY

281

Ruts can be comfortable places to stay. But life is dynamic. Growth and change are a constant part of each day. Give change a chance to transform tomorrow into something even more beautiful.

WHAT YOU FEEL MAY (OR MAY NOT) BE REAL

282

Your emotions are not an accurate measure of truth. Pay attention to them. Just be aware that they can be a fickle guide. Balance them with common sense, advice from those you trust, past experience and a good dose of prayer.

IT'S EASY TO SAY
"KEEP YOUR PRIORITIES STRAIGHT"

Balancing what's important with what's urgent gets tricky at times. When making commitments, keep your true priorities in mind—what's worth living for and dying for. The rest is simply the business end of life.

283

CHECK YOUR POWER SOURCE

Want true balance in your life? Plug yourself in spiritually, relationally and physically to what energizes you most. It takes all three to keep you strong and steady.

284

"THOSE WHO BRING SUNSHINE TO
THE LIVES OF OTHERS CANNOT KEEP
IT FROM THEMSELVES."
James Matthew Barrie

Giving love away never leaves you with less. It expands your heart so it can hold even more. Let love enlarge your life.

285

286
RIDE THE COATTAILS OF SUCCESS
The best time to tackle tough stuff is when you're feeling on top of the world. That's when your confidence, commitment and resilience can help you power through. Don't rest on your laurels. Use them as fuel for future success.

287
DO COMMON THINGS UNCOMMONLY WELL
During the Renaissance, sculptors made certain their art was as perfect in back as in front—even though the back often remained unseen. The attention you pay to small things says a lot about how you'll handle what's truly important.

288
RELISH YOUR RELATIONSHIPS
Give yourself a personal pick-me-up by flipping through your mental scrapbook. Bring to mind those who are closest to your heart. Thank God for the love in your life.

"START BY DOING WHAT'S NECESSARY,
THEN WHAT'S POSSIBLE
AND SUDDENLY YOU ARE DOING
THE IMPOSSIBLE."

Francis of Assisi

289

What's out of reach today may be within your grasp tomorrow. Potential always pushes the boundaries of "possible."

FINDING THE MISSING PEACE

290

You can have broken places in your life, yet still be whole. Invite God to help you find balance and beauty in both sunshine and shadow. Wholeness is at the heart of God's plans for you.

A FRUIT INSPECTION
CAN BE SWEET

291

A full life is a fruitful life. What you produce in the lives of others (love, laughter, joy, generosity, kindness, etc.) you'll find you harvest in your own.

292

"HAPPINESS IS NOT A STATE
TO ARRIVE AT,
BUT A MANNER OF TRAVELING."
Margaret Lee Runbeck
The lighter the heart, the less circumstances
can weigh you down. Hold tightly to the good
and loosely to the rest.

293

TAME YOUR INNER PACK RAT
Teapots, figurines, rare books… there are
countless things to "collect" in this world.
Appreciate the novelty of an item without
actually purchasing it. Try collecting memories,
instead. They're less expensive and take up
a lot less space.

IS WHAT'S EATING YOU
CHOOSING WHAT YOU EAT?

All of your relationships are important. But if food is your comforter, counselor and friend, it's time to break up. Food nourishes your body. It can't nourish your soul. Deal with the real problem or food will become one.

294

THE SEARCH FOR SIGNIFICANCE
IS INSIGNIFICANT

You don't have to hunt for what you already have. Recognition may come from things like status, titles and achievements. But significance was yours at birth. You're eternally, irrevocably, undeniably important. Rest in that truth.

295

WHAT YOU SAY ABOUT OTHERS
SAYS A LOT ABOUT YOU

296

Go ahead. Talk about others' behind their back. Just say something nice. If you have a problem with someone, talk to that person directly. It can keep little problems from turning into big ones.

"IF YOU CANNOT SERVE,
YOU CANNOT RULE."
Proverb

297

A great leader is an empathetic leader. Don't just strive to understand what it's like to walk in the shoes of those who follow you, but put on those shoes when the opportunity arises.

"A GRACIOUS WOMAN RETAINS HONOR"
Proverbs 11:16 NIV

298

Traits like power and prestige command respect. Kindness doesn't command. It encourages. Embrace the best in others, providing an environment that promotes growth. Mutual respect will bloom at the same time.

A MISTAKE IS EVIDENCE YOU TRIED

299

The only way to guarantee you'll never fail is to never try. Of course, that also guarantees you'll never succeed. Even a step forward that begins with a step back is a step worth taking.

CHARACTER SPEAKS
LOUDER THAN WORDS

300
Your reputation can be tarnished by untruths others say about you. But no one can tarnish your character, except you. Let the best of you shine through.

REGARDLESS OF THE PAST,
THE FUTURE'S UNWRITTEN

301
Everyone has a past. Everyone also has the clean slate of tomorrow. Give yourself and those around you the opportunity to write a different storyline than what's expected.

SWEET DREAMS REQUIRE
SWEET SLUMBER

302

There's always more you can do. Adequate rest helps you do it well. Sleep is an investment in tomorrow. Invest wisely by doing all you can to ensure a good night's sleep.

EVEN AN OPEN BOOK KEEPS SOME
THINGS UNDERCOVER

303

Being open and honest doesn't obligate you to reveal every detail of your life. Share what's necessary with those you deem trustworthy. The rest is between you and God.

304

"GOD GAVE US MEMORY THAT WE MIGHT HAVE ROSES IN DECEMBER."
James Matthew Barrie

Recalling the celebratory summer moments of life are a reminder that every winter comes to an end. Hang in there. Roses will bloom in your life again.

305

REALITY IS NOT A SHOW

Movies and TV are fine for entertainment. But their picture of life, love, sex, communication, and even a normal body weight, are far from reality. If you feel down on your own life after watching them, find a more positive pastime.

306

AN INTIMIDATION EVALUATION AIDS THE SITUATION

Intimidated? Determine whether you're afraid, in awe or inadequate. Is that root feeling justified or just runaway emotion? Identifying why you're feeling the way you do can help you better plan how to do what needs to be done.

"WHEN LOVE AND SKILL WORK TOGETHER, EXPECT A MASTERPIECE."
John Ruskin

A work of heart creates a work of art. Consider where your passion and ability intersect. Look for opportunities to explore and expand that sweet spot.

307

HOLIDAYS SHOULD BE HAPPY DAYS

Family traditions can be heartwarming…or stress-inducing. If they shift from blessings to burdens, rethink them. Be the generation that inspires a new kind of celebration.

308

PAUSE FOR PANORAMAS

Life's like a road trip. Sometimes, you've just got to pull over and look at the scenery. You'll never pass this day again. Take a break and enjoy the view!

309

HOLD YOUR HEAD UP

310

Regardless of whether you're on top of the world or in the throes of a meltdown, you have so much to give. So, put your chin up. Look others in the eye. Do your very best. You've got what it takes to tackle today.

"GOD OFTEN VISITS US, BUT MOST OF THE TIME WE'RE NOT AT HOME."
Joseph Roux

311

When you feel that nudge to act, that twinge of conscience guiding you a different direction or that whisper that says you're deeply loved, listen. God may be making a house call.

EXERCISE YOUR VOCABULARY

312

Want to feel better, sleep better and keep your brain working at its best? Get some exercise. If just hearing the word makes you sweat, choose a different word. Dance. Garden. Vacuum. Hike. Bike. Golf... Choose a word that moves you.

POPULARITY IS A PASSING FAD

Friends are more important than fans. It isn't the breadth, but the depth, of your relationships that makes them worthwhile.

313

THERE'S NO "IOU" IN HELP

Attach wings, instead of strings, to every favor you do for others. Don't just lend a hand. Give it away.

314

"FEAR MAKES THE WOLF BIGGER THAN HE IS."
Proverb

Emotion can act like a magnifying glass, distorting the true size of things. Sort the rational from the irrational before making your next move.

315

IT'S TOUGH TO WEIGH AN OPPORTUNITY

316
You never know where an open door will lead. The little thing you say "yes" to today may lead to even bigger, brighter prospects tomorrow. When opportunity knocks, answer.

"IF INSTEAD OF A GEM, OR EVEN A FLOWER, WE SHOULD CAST THE GIFT OF A LOVING THOUGHT INTO THE HEART OF A FRIEND, THAT WOULD BE GIVING AS THE ANGELS GIVE."
George MacDonald

317
Give those you love something they can hold in their hearts, instead of their hands…a carefully chosen word.

DECLARE EMANCIPATION DAY

318
What is enslaving you? Debt? Fear? A destructive habit? Let today be the day you get serious about becoming a free woman. The only fight you can win is one that actually begins.

THE FLIP SIDE OF EMOTION

Feelings get a bad rap for often being irrational and erratic. But they can also be the spark that fires you up to do something your brain says can't be done. It's okay to lead with your heart, as long as your head doesn't totally get left behind.

319

"AN HONEST ANSWER IS LIKE A KISS ON THE LIPS."
Proverbs 24:26 NIV

You can be candid and caring at the same time. When love and truth work together to deliver a difficult message it's harder to rebuff and easier to receive.

320

EXERCISE YOUR BRAIN AND INSPIRE YOUR HEART

Commit inspirational words to memory—such as a poem, quotation or verse of scripture. Lift your spirits anytime, anywhere by bringing it to mind.

321

DISAGREE WITHOUT
BEING DISAGREEABLE

322

Say what you mean. Mean what you say. And if you can't think of a positive way to respond, ask questions. Honest ones. Then, listen carefully. You don't have to accept what others say or believe to accept who they are.

"THE FIRST HOUR IS THE
RUDDER OF THE DAY."
Henry Ward Beecher

323

There's no right or wrong side of the bed to wake up on. What matters is how you choose to greet the day. Ample time to get ready, a healthy breakfast and an attitude of prayer make for a positive wake-up call.

HEREDITY IS JUST
A BUILDING BLOCK

324

Privilege or problem, you choose how to use everything you receive—including what you received at birth. Your legacy will speak louder than your heredity. Choose carefully what you'd like it to say.

"FORGIVENESS IS THE FRAGRANCE THAT THE VIOLET SHEDS ON THE HEEL THAT HAS CRUSHED IT."
Mark Twain

325

Forgiveness doesn't ignore or excuse an offense. It grants a full pardon. It also grants you the power to let go of any grudge that's weighing you down.

YOU CAN'T GET WHAT YOU WANT 'TIL YOU KNOW WHAT IT IS

326

Complaining comes easy. Fixing what you're whining about takes work. First, figure out what you're really longing for. Second, figure out your part in helping to fill that need. Third, do your part.

SEEK OUT ADVERSITY

327

Read true-life stories about people who've overcome major obstacles in their lives. Their personal conquests can spark creativity, perseverance and gratitude in your own life.

SOMETIMES IT PAYS
TO DISCOUNT A DISCOUNT

328

Sales, coupons and the deal of the day only save you money if you intend to purchase the item anyway. If not, they can trick you into spending by convincing you you're saving. You can't afford to buy into this kind of bargain.

A LITTLE FISH IN A BIG POND
HAS A LOT OF ROOM TO GROW

329

If you're low woman on the totem pole, look up. Learn from those above you. Keep in mind how your work is integral to overall success. Doing small jobs with the same excellence you do large ones is what makes you a leader at any level.

USE DOWNTIME
TO BUILD YOURSELF UP

You can do something big—like write a novel, learn Mandarin or earn a degree—even if you have little free time. Spare moments add up. Use them as stepping stones to reach your dreams.

330

"WE CANNOT HELP CONFORMING
OURSELVES TO WHAT WE LOVE."
Frances de Sales

Choose your friends wisely. Those we admire, we tend to imitate. Hang out with people whose habits you'd be happy to call your own.

331

THERE'S ONLY ONE YOU

Like every person, you have three sides: who you want people to think you are, who you think you are and who you really are. When those three are identical, that's when you're a balanced individual.

332

HIDE AND SEEK

333

Leisure is a resting place. Laziness is a hiding place. If your get-up-and-go is gone, don't berate yourself. Figure out what you're afraid of—and how you're going to face it.

USE IT OR LOSE IT

334

When you learn something new, make it stick by acting on what you now know. Put it into practice. Teach it to others. Blog about it. The more you bring it to mind, the more easily it will stay there.

"GOD DIVIDED THE HAND INTO FINGERS SO THAT MONEY WOULD SLIP THROUGH."
Martin Luther

335

The more you practice giving, the better you get at it. Bless those around you with the blessings you've received!

FEEL AT HOME WHEN
YOU'RE ALONE

Friendship is fabulous. But those you love can't complete you. You're already whole. Being comfortable with yourself includes being comfortable by yourself.

336

DEAL WITH THE DETAILS

Loose ends are like shoe laces. If you don't tie them up, they'll trip you up. Take care of the small stuff so it never has the chance to turn into big stuff.

337

CHANGE NUMBERS TO NAMES

It's hard to relate to statistics about social issues like hunger or homelessness. Put a face on that number, someone you deeply love. When it's someone you know, even "one" is enough to move you to action.

338

WHILE MAKING A LIVING
MAKE ROOM FOR A LIFE

339

After I get that promotion… When the kids are grown… Once I retire… It's easy to put off what doesn't help pay the bills. But there's no pause button on life. Love it as you live it.

"THERE IS NOTHING MORE
BEAUTIFUL THAN CHEERFULNESS
IN AN OLD FACE."
Jean Paul Richter

340

Regardless of your age, a smile is your best accessory. The more joy and love you purposefully share with others, the more that smile will grow.

YOU ARE CHOSEN

Your circle of friends—and you know what great taste they have—picked you to love. That's quite an honor. It's also one more reminder of just what a wonderful woman you are.

341

KNOW WHEN TO PUT SACRED COWS OUT TO PASTURE

Even what's tried and true can become obsolete. Shake things up now. Make certain the way you're doing them is still the best way for them to be done.

342

FOOD FOR THOUGHT

Your mind is like a fine meal. The ingredients you put in season the finished product. What you set your mind on will flavor your life. Choose wisely.

343

CONFIDENCE COMES FROM DOING WHAT YOU THINK YOU CAN'T

344

Doing what's easy is, well, easy. It isn't an accomplishment. It's a no-brainer. The tough stuff is what let's you know what you're really made of. Go for it. Challenge your confidence to get up and get growing.

"SILENCES MAKE THE REAL CONVERSATIONS BETWEEN FRIENDS."
Margaret Lee Runbeck

345

A relationship that's comfortable with quiet has moved beyond expectations and entertainment to genuine devotion. Just being there is enough.

ON THE BEST BLESSED LIST

346

Counting your blessings sounds so cliché. Yet there's nothing trite about the wealth of good gifts you've been given—starting with life itself. Contentment and gratitude grow as you become more aware of all you received.

LOVE YOUR FRIENDS
BY LOVING YOURSELF

Do those you love a favor. Take care of
yourself. Wear sunscreen. Buckle your seatbelt.
Schedule your annual check-up. You, and your
health, matter to those around you.

347

UNDERCOVER OPERATION

Even while you're sleeping your brain is at
work solving and sorting. Keep a notepad on
your nightstand. Jot down thoughts that keep
you awake or greet you first thing in the morning.
Your brain may be trying to tell you something.

348

"NO ONE TESTS THE DEPTH OF A
RIVER WITH BOTH FEET."
Proverb

Enthusiasm is a great asset. But prudence
is its practical partner. When the two work
together, every endeavor of yours has a greater
chance of success.

349

WITH THE RIGHT TENSION, YARN CAN BECOME A SWEATER

350

Stress is a natural push and pull of life. It pushes you to meet a deadline or pulls you toward bed after you've put in a long day. Like many things, it's beneficial in moderation. Listen to what stress is telling you—loosen up or get moving.

HOLD ONTO HOPE

351

Every day is sunny. But sometimes clouds get in the way, obscuring what's true. When storms gather in your life, take heart. There's more at work in this life than what you can see with your eyes.

THE DRIVING FORCE INSIDE YOU

352

The driver's seat is like a polygraph. It doesn't allow you to hide the truth. It can bring out the best, or worst, in you. Pay attention to not only the road, but to who you are behind the wheel. Fine-tune as needed.

THANK A TEACHER

Professor, parent, neighbor, friend, mentor, minister, author…so many people have taught you so much through the years. Their wealth of knowledge has helped enrich your life.

353

"I AM SEEKING, I AM STRIVING, I AM IN IT WITH ALL MY HEART."
Vincent Van Gogh

Once you say you're in, be all the way in. Only make commitments you're ready to live up to.

354

THE STARS SHINE MORE BRIGHTLY IN THE EVENING OF LIFE

As time passes, it brings to light what's most important. As soon as you notice something is trivial, wasteful or petty, cast it off. Choose to travel light into the days ahead.

355

YOU CAN'T MAKE TIME; YOU HAVE TO TAKE IT

356

Too bad you can't whip up an extra batch of time to keep in the freezer for emergencies. Unfortunately, taking time to do one thing means forfeiting time for something else. Weigh what you're giving up against what you're gaining.

THINKING IT THROUGH

357

It's okay to change your mind. Time, experience and the insight of others, will put your choices, opinions and beliefs to the test. That's a good thing. They should be tested and found true. Only then can you live what you believe with conviction.

"GOODNESS THAT PREACHES UNDOES ITSELF."
Ralph Waldo Emerson

358

Your actions speak for themselves. Sweetening your deeds with your own words is like adding too much sugar when baking a cake. The result is hard to swallow.

GOOD FRIENDS ARE ADEPT AT BACKBENDS

359

When a friend rearranges her schedule or goes out of her way to accommodate you in some way, love is hard at work. How flexible are you at bending over backward to help others in need?

BE PATIENT WITH YOURSELF

360

Growth takes time. Your entire life is a process of becoming, of maturing, of learning to deeply love so you can wholly live. Celebrate each new bud of growth, trusting each one will blossom in due time.

WITHOUT RESOLVE, RESOLUTIONS ARE JUST WISHES

361

Think it. Plan it. Declare it. Act on it. Then get up and do it all over again the next day… and the next. That's how what you resolve you'd like to do becomes something you're proud you did.

TURN SMALL TALK INTO A SCAVENGER HUNT

362

When chit-chatting at social gatherings, forget about yourself. Focus on others. Move beyond the basics. Ask about defining moments in their lives, their hopes and dreams. Even if you never meet again, your time will be well spent.

IT TAKES A GREAT WOMAN
TO BECOME SMALL

363

You may be the CEO of a large company. But there still may be a time when you're called on to clean toilets. No job is below a truly great woman. She rises to every task, even when she has to stoop to do it.

"MY BEST FRIEND IS THE ONE WHO
BRINGS OUT THE BEST IN ME."
Henry Ford

364

Be a powerful force in you friends' lives. Your love, acceptance and honesty can help bring to light how amazing they truly are. Share it freely.

THE FUTURE UNFOLDS
ONE DAY AT A TIME

365

Want a brighter future? Shine. Let the world see your distinctive beauty and experience first-hand the depth of the love that continues to grow in your heart. Give yourself away…today.

The LORD bless thee,
and keep thee.
Numbers 6:24